ULTIMATE MILITARY MACHINES

FIGHTER PLANES

Tim Cooke

A$^+$

Smart Apple Media

This edition published in 2013 by
Smart Apple Media, an imprint of Black Rabbit Books
PO Box 3263, Mankato, MN 56002

www.blackrabbitbooks.com

Brown Bear Books Ltd.
Editorial Director: Lindsey Lowe
Managing Editor: Tim Cooke
Children's Publisher: Anne O'Daly
Picture Manager: Sophie Mortimer
Creative Director: Jeni Child

Library of Congress Cataloging-in-Publication Data

Fighter planes / edited by Tim Cooke.
     p. cm. -- (Ultimate military machines)
 Includes index.
 Audience: Grades 4-6.
 ISBN 978-1-59920-820-6 (library binding)
 1. Fighter planes--Juvenile literature. I. Cooke, Tim, 1961-
 UG1242.F5F52 2013
 623.74'64--dc23
                          2012007408

Printed in the United States of America at Corporate Graphics, North Mankato, Minnesota

Picture Credits

Front Cover: U.S. Airforce

BAe Sytems: 28tr; John Batchelor: 06/07; Bundesheer: 29br; Coert van Breda: 27tc; Corel: 05bl; Robert Hunt Library: 05tr,
06bl, 08, 17tl, 17cr, 20, 21; U.S. Airforce: 04, 06cl, 09bl, 09br, 11cl, 11bl, 13tr, 14c, 22tc, 27bl; U.S. Department of
Defense: 07br, 10, 11tr, 12/13, 13bl, 14br, 15b, 16, 18/19, 18b, 19b, 22br, 23, 24, 25tr, 25b, 26bl, 28bl; U.S. Marine
Corps: 09tl, 15tr; U.S. Navy: 17bl, 26tr, 29tr.

Key: t = top, c =center, b = bottom, l = left, r = right.

All Artworks: Windmill Books.

PO1438
2-2012

9 8 7 6 5 4 3 2 1

CONTENTS

INTRODUCTION

The fighter plane is key to modern combat. Fast and easy to maneuver, it attacks enemies in the air. From the ground, the loops and rolls of the top guns are visible only as vapor trails.

● STEALTH

One-man crew in cockpit

Engines buried inside the wings

SPECIFICATIONS
Crew: 1
Wingspan: 43.3 ft (13.2 m)
Max Speed: 617 mph (993 km/h)
Armament: 2 internal bays for up to 4,000 lb (1,815 kg) of bombs

NIGHTHAWK

The F-117 Nighthawk is part-fighter, part-strike aircraft. It is the latest in technology. Hidden from radar, it can get through defenses to surprise the enemy.

RADAR: A system that uses radio waves to find the location of objects.

EARLY DAYS

Before World War I, the cavalry worried that aircraft would scare their horses. The planes were used for observation. But military planners could already see their potential as weapons.

▲ A squadron of U.S. Army World War I biplanes (planes with two sets of wings). Pilots who shot down many enemy fighters were called "aces."

WORLD WAR I

In World War I (1914–1918) scout aircraft flew above the trenches to spy on the enemy. Each carried a pilot and an observer. To begin with, the observers fired rifles at any enemy scouts. Soon, the aircraft were fitted with machine guns.

WORLD WAR II

At the start of World War II (1939–1945), Germany used blitzkrieg tactics to conquer much of Europe. Ju 87 Stuka dive bombers and Heinkel 111s struck airfields and cities. Blitzkrieg tactics depended on quickly winning control of the skies to dominate the enemy.

◀ A German Me109 and a British Spitfire (top). The planes fought the Battle of Britain in 1940.

BLITZKRIEG: A German word that means "lightning war."

WHAT IS A FIGHTER?

A fighter is a military airplane designed to destroy the enemy in the air. Fighters are lightning fast, and easy to turn in tight twists or loops. Modern fighters carry a combination of machine guns, rockets, and missiles. They also use bombs to strike targets on the ground.

AIR-TO-AIR MISSILES

AD
AF 83 123

◄ An F-16 Fighting Falcon fires an AIM 120 air-to-air missile. A fighter's main job is to destroy enemy fighters.

AERIAL DUEL

Vapor shows the trail of enemy fighters in a dogfight in World War II. Each pilot tried to get the other in his sights to shoot at while not getting shot down himself.

Four cannon mounted in nose

DOGFIGHT: A one-on-one, close-range clash between two fighters.

FIRST FIGHTER

World War II saw a race for fighter power. Late in the war, Germany produced the Messerschmitt Me 262. It was the first jet fighter. It could fly higher and faster and climb more quickly than propeller-driven planes. But it came too late to change the outcome of the war.

Swastika, symbol of the Nazis

ME 262

Aerodynamic cockpit canopy

Swept-back wings increase speed

Jet engines draw air into turbines

▶ U.S. F-16 Fighting Falcons fly in formation. Formations allow fighters to protect one another from attack.

AERODYNAMIC: Designed so that air passes easily over a surface.

FIGHTER ROLE

A fighter's traditional job has been to defend airspace. Its key method of defense is attack. It strikes enemy aircraft before they can gain air superiority. Today, fighters often have both defensive and offensive roles. They are called multirole combat aircraft (MRCA).

"The most important thing to a fighter pilot is speed. The faster an aircraft is moving when he spots the enemy, the sooner he will be able to take the bounce."
DUANE BEESON, MUSTANG PILOT, 1945

FRIENDS ABOVE

Vapor trails mark the paths of P-51 Mustang fighters escorting U.S. B-17 bombers to Germany in World War II. Bombers are often slow and vulnerable, so escort duties are a key fighter role.

TAKE THE BOUNCE: To get out of a situation.

SOUND BARRIER

Vapor bursts around a U.S. Navy F/A-18 Hornet as it breaks the sound barrier. Whatever weapons a fighter plane carries, its greatest weapon is still sheer speed.

"The first time I ever saw a jet, I shot it down."
CHUCK YAEGER, UNITED STATES AIR FORCE, ON MEETING AN ME 262.

SOUND AND BEYOND

The key part of a modern air force is the supersonic fighter, faster than the speed of sound. Modern MCRAs are highly adaptable. They are used in air-to-air combat, or for ground attack or bombing tasks.

▲ U.S. pilot Chuck Yaeger was the first man to break the sound barrier, in 1947. The U.S. soon began using supersonic fighters (left).

AIRBORNE POLICE

In times of threat, the Combat Air Patrol (CAP) gets off the ground. Its fighters look out for enemy intruders as a first line of defense. CAPs are common over areas where war seems imminent.

EAGLE EYES

The F-15 Eagle is a tactical fighter. Its job is to take out enemy aircraft and command centers. The pilot uses a heads-up visual display to aim guns and missiles.

▲ Two U.S. F-15s and an AT-38 fly on CAP over the desert in the Persian Gulf in the 1990s.

HEADS UP VISUAL DISPLAY: A visor that displays information.

PROTECTING THE PEOPLE

Fighters guard against air terror. In the attacks of September 11, 2001, terrorists used aircraft to attack New York City and Washington, DC. Under Operation Noble Eagle, fighters now patrol the skies 24 hours a day, protecting the United States.

▼ F-15 Eagles fly a CAP over the eastern seaboard of the United States.

F-117 NIGHTHAWK

NOBLE EAGLE

▼ F-15 Eagles fly a CAP over the eastern seaboard of the United States.

SIGHT UNSEEN

The F-117 Nighthawk is an attack fighter first flown in 1981. The stealthy Nighthawk can strike its targets without ever being "seen" by enemy radar.

COATING

◀ The Nighthawk is coated with a secret nonreflective material and flown with computerized controls.

FIGHTER FIREPOWER

The fighter plane is a hunter. It locates enemy aircraft and destroys them. At long range, modern planes use missiles; in close combat, cannons do the job. Fighter–bombers designed to strike ground targets carry air-to-ground missiles and bombs.

FULLY LOADED

The F-16 Fighting Falcon carries wingtip and rack missiles. The fighter was built to be unstable as it flies. It bounces around in the air, which actually makes it easier to maneuver.

SPECIFICATIONS

Crew: 1
Wingspan: 32.6 ft (9.96 m)
Max. speed: 1,500 mph
(2,410 km/h)
Armament: 1 cannon,
4 rocket, 4–6 missiles,
8 bombs

● F-16 FIGHTING FALCON

Fire-control radar in nose finds targets

Air intake for engine

CANNON: An automatic, heavy gun carried by an aircraft or tank.

GUIDANCE

Firing is not left to chance. Precision-guided missiles (PGMs) lock onto another aircraft, no matter how it tries to dodge. The precision systems work by radar or infrared technology.

SIDEWINDER

The Sidewinder air interception missile (AIM) is guided by infrared. It has a range of up to 11 miles (18 km). It is still one of the most effective short-range missiles.

◀ An F-16 pilot fires a Sidewinder from his wingtip. The Sidewinder is the most widely used missile in the West.

Wing rack for rockets

FIGHTER BOMBERS

MRCAs are not just designed to fight other aircraft. They can also strike targets on the ground. Airplanes like the F-16 Fighting Falcon carry guided missiles and bombs. The weapons are steered by laser or by video via the pilot's screen.

MAVERICK

An F-16 launches a Maverick air-to-ground missile. The missile's on-board camera is linked to a video screen in the cockpit. The pilot steers the missile to its target.

F-16 MISSILE

LASER ROCKET

An F-15 Eagle drops heat-seeking rockets. Sensors in the rockets' noses guide them precisely to their targets.

COCKPIT: The part of an aircraft where the pilot sits.

GUNS AND CANNONS

Modern fighters often carry high-speed 20 mm Gatling guns. They are designed for close-range combat, so are rarely used. Modern air warfare is fought at longer range, so pilots rely more on missiles.

EYEWITNESS

"In combat flying, precision aerobatic work is really not of much use. It is the rough maneuver that succeeds."
"BUBI" HARTMANN, GERMAN ACE, WWII

WORLD WAR II ACE

U.S. pilot Gregory "Pappy" Boyington shot down at least 22 enemy planes in World War II. He was the Marine Corps' top-scoring ace in the conflict. He later led the famous Black Sheep Squadron.

• P-47 THUNDERBOLT

▲ A P-47 Thunderbolt fires its wing guns at night in World War II.

GATLING GUN: A machine gun with multiple rotating barrels.

FIGHTER CREW

From World War I aces to high-tech aircrew, pilots have been seen as lone warriors high above the earth. But in modern conflict, teamwork and coordination between the air and the ground are vital.

TEAM AT WORK

A modern fighter cockpit is a communications center. Pilots talk constantly to air controllers or with other pilots on the same mission. Wherever they are, fighter pilots are never alone.

G-SUITS

For high-altitude, high-speed combat, fighter pilots wear heated G-suits. The coveralls have features to prevent the loss of blood from the head during combat moves.

G-SUIT: Coveralls designed to resist the effects of gravity (g-force or "G").

WORLD WAR I

In World War I, fighter cockpits were open to the weather. Pilots wore fur-lined leather coats for warmth. Their heads and eyes were protected by a tight leather helmet and goggles.

WORLD WAR II

Although cockpits in World War II were enclosed, pilots still wore thick clothes against the cold. They often wore life jackets, in case they had to ditch at sea.

VIRTUAL REALITY

Modern pilots train in simulators. They can practice maneuvers or fight the enemy above accurate images of real landscapes.

EYEWITNESS

"When you've flown a mission in these simulators, it's a 'been there, done that' sort of thing when it's time for the actual mission."
INSTRUCTOR, LANGLEY AIR FORCE BASE

DITCH: To crash-land an aircraft at sea.

FIGHTER TACTICS

The skill of a pilot under pressure determines how well a fighter plane performs. To make sure a pilot is always at his best, pilots train and practice continually. Some of the combat tactics they use have not changed since World War I.

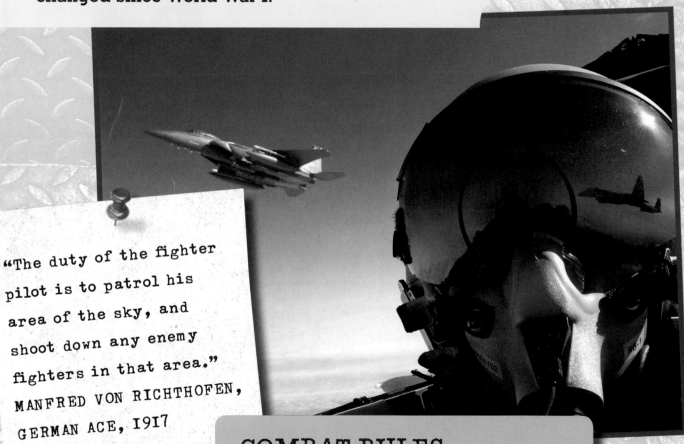

"The duty of the fighter pilot is to patrol his area of the sky, and shoot down any enemy fighters in that area."
MANFRED VON RICHTHOFEN, GERMAN ACE, 1917

COMBAT RULES

Since World War I, a pilot has learned three basic rules: to attack from above and behind; to keep watching the sky; and to guard against attacks out of the sun.

FIRE CONTROL: Systems that keep guns and missiles locked on target.

◀ F-16s have powerful fire control radars that map the ground and can lock on to up to 10 targets at a time.

ELECTRONICS

In modern warfare pilots rely on the latest technology to seek out and hit a target while in flight. The enemy can be out of sight but radar will locate him. The pilot can then activate guided missiles that lock-on. They travel at Mach 4—up to four times faster than the speed of sound, or about 2,500 mph (4,000 km/h).

WINGMAN

A pilot's best friend is his wingman. The wingman flies behind and outside the lead aircraft. His job is to protect the leader from enemy coming in from behind or from the side.

▲ Three U.S. F-15s fly in a V-shape. This formation allows the lead jet to seek out enemy targets, while the other aircraft protect it from flank attacks.

LOCK-ON: When a missile is fixed on its target and guided toward it.

FIGHTER HISTORY

Since the early fighter planes of World War I, many things have changed in fighter technology: the planes, the training, the missiles, and the gear. But the job remains the same—to destroy enemy aircraft and defend the skies.

MUSTANG MARVEL

The North American P-51 Mustang was one of the star performers of World War II, helping to defeat the Luftwaffe. The long-range escort fighters protected Allied bombers on raids over Germany. They cut casualties among the heavy bombers.

SPECIFICATIONS

Crew: 1
Wingspan: 37 ft (11.3 m)
Max Speed: 437 mph (702 km/h)
Ceiling: 42,000 ft (12,800 m)
Armament: 6 x 0.5 in. Browning machine guns

LUFTWAFFE: The name of the German air force.

WORLD WAR II

The early U.S. bombers that flew over Germany were slow and easy targets for fast German fighters. The P-51 Mustang changed that. It was fast and could fly at high altitudes, making it an ideal escort fighter.

ANTIAIRCRAFT

Antiaircraft artillery provides the best defense against low-flying fighter–bomber attacks. Here, U.S. Marines fire on Japanese fighters during World War II.

302

315

USMC

EYEWITNESS

"We soon found out that the P-5I Mustang was indeed a different breed of airplane. It was fast, for one thing..."
ROBERT GOEBEL, GERMAN FIGHTER PILOT

JOHN GLENN, JR.

Senator John H. Glenn, Jr., the first astronaut to orbit the Earth, was a fighter pilot in World War II and Korea (1950–1953). He won many medals for bravery, shooting down three MiGs.

MIG: A Russian-built fighter plane.

KOREAN WAR

During the Korean War (1950–1953) jet fighters were used for the first time. U.S. F-86 Sabres, backing the United Nations and South Korea, fought Soviet-built MiG 15s, supporting North Korea, to control the skies above "MiG Alley."

▼ John Glenn's F-86 Sabre in Korea carried the words "MiG Mad Marine." Glenn shot down three MiGs.

● F-86 SABRE

AIR SUPREMACY

After Korea, the U.S. developed the F-105 Thunderchief. This fighter–bomber was used extensively in the Vietnam War.

UNITED NATIONS: A body for resolving international disputes.

LIBYA

In 1981 Libya's then-leader Mummar El-Qaddafi announced that he wanted to extend Libyan territory up to 12 miles (19 km) into the Mediterranean Sea. That would have broken international law. U.S. aircraft carriers were sent to stop the Libyan advance.

Body made from light but strong titanium

Weapon load of up to 15,000 lb (6,800 kg)

Nose contains aviation electronics

Two-man cockpit with ejector seats

F-14 TOMCAT

TOMCATS FIGHT BACK

On August 19, 1981, two Libyan Su-22s attacked two F-14 Tomcats near Libya. One fired an Atoll missile at the Tomcats. It failed to explode but the Tomcats hit back. They quickly shot down both Su-22s. The U.S. show of aerial strength meant that Libya could not go through with the planned extension of its borders.

EJECTOR SEAT: A safety seat that propels a pilot out of a plane.

23

FALKLANDS WAR

In April 1982 Argentina occupied the British-owned Falkland Islands, just off the Argentine coast. The British sent a naval task force to the South Atlantic. Hawker Sea Harriers destroyed at least 20 enemy fighters and established air superiority. That allowed an amphibious landing to take place. The Argentines surrendered after two-and-a-half months' fighting.

▼ The British Hawker Sea Harrier served in the Falklands War, both Gulf Wars, and the Balkans conflict in the 1990s.

SEA HARRIER

The British only had one fighter capable of flying from the Royal Navy's VSTOL carriers: the Hawker Sea Harrier. In the two-month conflict, British pilots flew 1,435 missions with no losses.

VSTOL: Vertical/short takeoff and landing.

DESERT STORM

During the 1991 Persian Gulf War, Coalition forces fought back against the Iraqi invasion of neighboring Kuwait. Fighters led by the United States carried out more than 100,000 sorties. They targeted both military and civilian targets.

▲ A U.S. F-16 leaves its base in Europe in 2011 to take up position in Iraq.

MIG DOWN

A MiG fighter lies in ruins after being shot down during the first Gulf War. Russian-built MiGs were used extensively by the Iraqis, but were slow and easy to attack.

SORTIE: A word used to describe an individual military flight or mission.

25

GALLERY

Fighter planes are extremely fast and relatively small with only one or two crew members. They are the best defense any air force can have. Fighters can destroy an enemy far away.

F-35 LIGHTNING II

SPECIFICATIONS
Crew: 1
Wingspan: 35 ft (10.7 m)
Max Speed: 1,200 mph
 (1,930 km/h)
Armament: 4-barrel
 gatling cannon

The F-35 is becoming the most important multirole fighter of the U.S. Air Force. It offers ground attack, air defense, and reconnaissance.

F-117 NIGHTHAWK

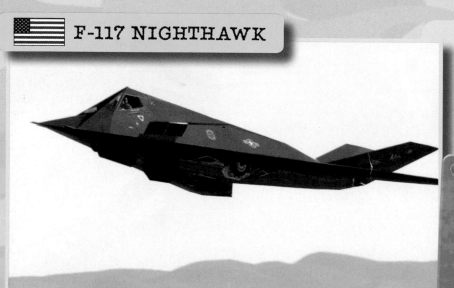

The F-117 was a ground-attack airplane built in the 1980s. It was the first fighter to use stealth technology. Only 59 went into service.

SPECIFICATIONS
Crew: 1
Wingspan: 43.3 ft (13.2 m)
Max Speed: 617 mph (993 km/h)
Armament: 2 bombs, including
 nuclear bombs

RECONNAISSANCE: Secretly gathering information about the enemy.

SPECIFICATIONS

Crew: 1

Wingspan: 37.4 ft (11.4 m)

Max Speed: 1,490 mph
(2,400 km/h).

Armament: 1 x 30mm
cannon, up to 7,720lb
(3,500 kg) of ordnance

The MiG 29 Fulcrum is the fourth generation of Russian-built all-weather fighters. In service since 1983, it is the equivalent of the F-15 and F/A-18. It is widely used around the world.

F-22 RAPTOR

The Raptor entered service in 2005. The fighter uses stealth technology, and is suited to ground-attack or electronic warfare roles, as well as air-to-air fighting.

SPECIFICATIONS

Crew: 1

Wingspan: 44.5 ft
(13.56 m)

Max Speed: 1,500 mph
(2,410 km/h)

Armament: 6-barrel
gatling cannon

ORDNANCE: Shells and other ammunition carried by an aircraft.

GALLERY

 MIRAGE 2000

The Dassault-Breguet Mirage 2000 is a multirole single-engine jet fighter used by the French air force. It has seen action in the Gulf Wars, Bosnia, and Kosovo. In 2011 it was used to enforce a no-fly zone over Libya.

SPECIFICATIONS
Crew: 1
Wingspan: 29 ft (9.13 m)
Max Speed: 1,500+ mph (2,530+ km/h)
Armament: 2 x 30mm revolver cannons; up to 8,820 lb (4000 kg) ordnance

GR4 TORNADO

SPECIFICATIONS
Crew: 2
Wingspan: 45.9 ft (13.99 m)
Max Speed: 1,490 mph (2,400 km/h)
Armament: 1 x 27mm revolver cannon; up to 19,800 lb (9,000 kg) payload

The Tornado is a multirole British fighter. The angle of its wing sweep can be varied by the pilot for maximum performance.

NO-FLY ZONE: An area over which aircraft are forbidden to fly.

The French-built Rafale
169 is a multirole
fighter. It was used
during the Libyan Civil
War of 2011 to enforce
the UN no-fly zone.

RAFALE 169

SPECIFICATIONS
Crew: 1–2
Wingspan: 35.4 ft (10.8 m)
Max Speed: 1,324 mph
   (2,130 km/h)
Armament: 1x30mm cannon;
   upto 21,000 lb (9,500 kg)
   ordnance

EUROFIGHTER

SPECIFICATIONS
Crew: 1 or 2
Wingspan: 35.7 ft (10.9 m)
Max Speed: 1,550 mph
   (2,495 km/h)
Armament: 1 x 27mm
   revolver cannon; up to
   16,500 lb (7,500 kg) payload

The Eurofighter is a multirole fighter that was
developed jointly by several European air forces.
It has been in use since 2003.

PAYLOAD: How much an aircraft can carry in addition to its crew.

GLOSSARY

aerodynamic Designed so that air passes easily over a surface.

airspace The part of the sky above a particular country.

blitzkrieg A German word that means "lightning war."

cannon An automatic, heavy gun carried by an aircraft or tank.

cockpit The part of an aircraft where the pilot sits.

ditch To crash-land an aircraft at sea.

dogfight A one-on-one, close-range clash between two fighters.

ejector seat A seat with a parachute that lifts a pilot out of a plane.

fire control Systems that keep guns and missiles locked on target.

gatling gun A machine gun with multiple rotating barrels.

G-suit Overalls designed to resist the effects of high gravity ("G").

heads up visual display A visor that displays information.

infrared Guided by invisible waves, usually generated by heat.

lock-on When a missile is fixed on its target and guided toward it.

Luftwaffe The name of the German air force.

MiG A Russian-built fighter plane.

no-fly zone An area over which aircraft are forbidden to fly.

nonreflective Material that does not bounce back radar signals.

ordnance Shells and other ammunition carried by an aircraft.

payload How much an aircraft can carry in addition to its crew.

radar A system that uses radio waves to find the location of objects.

reconnaissance Secretly gathering information about the enemy.

sortie A word used to describe an individual military flight or mission.

sound barrier Faster than the speed of sound, 768 mph (1,235 km/h).

UN The United Nations, a body for resolving international disputes.

visual display A helmet with a visor that displays information.

VSTOL Vertical/short takeoff and landing.

FURTHER READING

● BOOKS

Alvarez, Carlos. *F-35 Lightning II* (Torque Books). Bellwether Media, 2010.

Bledsoe, Glen, and Karen Bledsoe. *Fighter Planes: Fearless Fliers* (Mighty Military Machines). Enslow Publishers Inc., 2006.

Braulick, Carrie A. *U.S. Air Force Fighters* (Edge Books). Capstone Press, 2006.

David, Jack. *F-16 Fighting Falcons* (Torque Books). Belwether Media, 2007.

Green, Michael, and Gladys Green. *Tactical Fighters: The F-15 Eagles* (Edge Books). Capstone Press, 2008.

Jackson, Robert. *101 Great Fighters* (The 101 Greatest Weapons of All Times). Rosen Publishing Group, 2010.

● WEBSITES

http://www.sr-71.org/aircraft
Military Aircraft information gallery with images and fact sheets.

http://military.discovery.com/technology/vehicles/fighters/fighters-intro.html
Military Channel guide to the Top 10 fighters of all times.

http://www.toptenz.net/top-10-fastest-military-airplanes.php
Videos of the world's fastest fighter planes.

http://science.howstuffworks.com/wwii-plane.htm
Howstuffworks page about fighter aircraft in World War II.

http://www.combataircraft.com/en/Military-Aircraft/fighter-attack/
Comprehensive guide to fighter and attack airplanes.

INDEX